TITANIA'S WISHING SPELLS

WEALTH
TITANIA HARDIE

QUADRILLE

For Gavrik and Gabriel

All the spells in this little book will attract greater financial reward and overall prosperity. They will not—on their own—make you rich as Croesus; however, they will help you to find the right positive frame of mind to attract good things financially.

The spells derive from a long tradition of wishing. In the past, the inclination to try to detect signs in nature that would prove propitious to the workings of any given day gave rise to a regime of wishing on a good omen. Suddenly certain unusual combinations of weather or objects would come together, and the occasion would betoken a special outcome. If the spirits were appeased, the outcome would be the desired one: the crops assured, the transaction favorable, and so on.

Whether or not spells work is a matter for the heart and soul, rather than rationale: my own feeling is that, if we invest enough mental energy and determination in the enactment of wishes and spells, we make them come true. The object, then, is to fix your mind strongly on the desired end, and put as much mental energy into it as you can.

I love wishing spells, and they work well for me. Enjoy them, and I wish you many good wishes.

Shoes #1

Shoes have always been associated with prosperity: the very owning of them separated rich from poor! There is a bridal custom of throwing shoes after the bride, but this wish spell is at least as old as the wedding tradition.

As you are starting a new job or launching a new business, let one of your "old shoes" follow you:

Find a beautiful but worn-out pair of shoes, and keep one at home, the other at your place of work. It is best if someone actually throws one shoe after you: have a friend toss the shoe towards you at your new desk or establishment.

Fill both the shoes with flower buds or petals—orange blossom was traditional, and peony flowers are also associated with prosperity. Depending on the shoe, you may be able to put florist's foam in it and fill it with a few fresh flowers each week.

Make a wish upon the shoe(s) for plenty in the work ahead; wish, in short, never to be down at heel.

Tie pretty ribbons around the shoes, and preserve them somewhere for growing luck with your business.

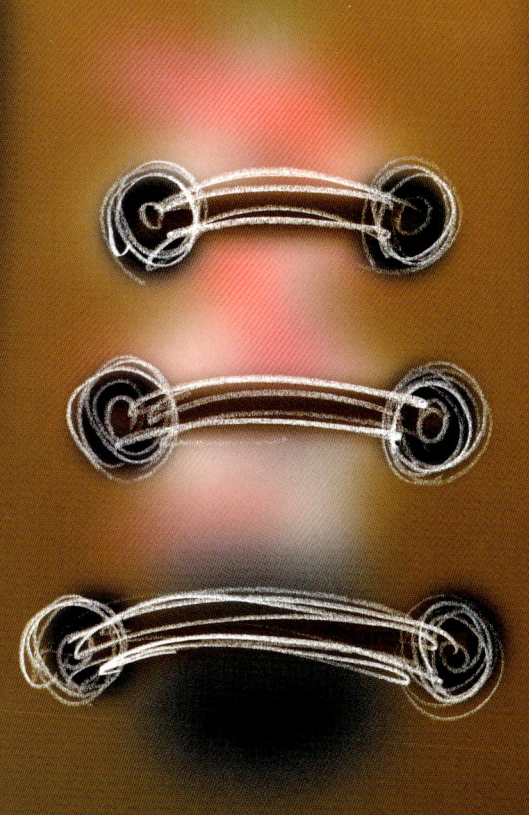

Shoes #2

After an especially lucky day, or a day which has been very good for business:

Take off your shoes, and hang the left one up either above your bed or beside a fireplace.

Stuff the shoe full of scented herbs, and say as you do so: "Keep my feet firm on the ground; but may the heights I reached today come oft again around." Now wish firmly for a future following again in the footsteps you took today.

In the morning, take a sprig from one of the herbs, and put it in a drawer where you keep money or account books. Your business and overall prosperity will reach greater heights.

Eggs

These have oft betokened prosperity, and many superstitions attach to eggs. They are very useful for making wishes for wealth.

If someone brings you eggs as a gift, or after doing the shopping for you, be sure to give them a small coin in return.

Take an egg from the box, picking one at random, and make sure you break the egg open at the large end. As you tap it, wish for prosperity and, if you like, wish on a very specific venture. Tap the egg exactly three times.

If you have been lucky enough to find a double-yolker, your wealth for the year is assured; but in any case, after you have used the egg, place some of the shell, crushed up, into a potted plant and grow a flower in it. Traditionally, it should be either a red geranium, or a yellow marigold.

You will be lucky with money, at least in little ways, from this day on.

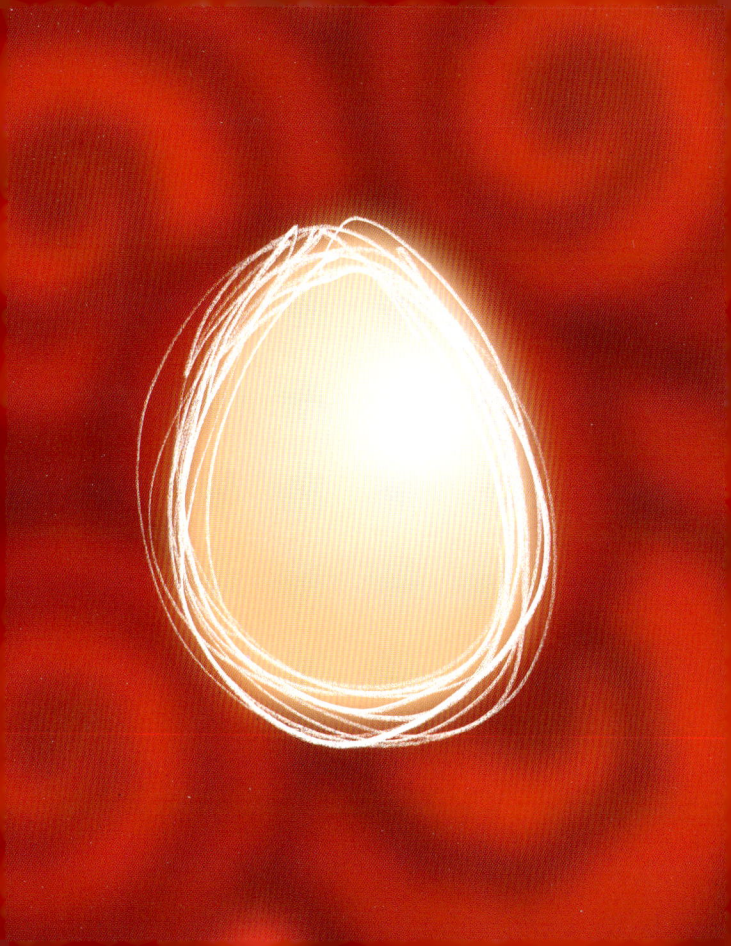

Dimples

These expression marks are thought to portend one's manner of earning money. "A dimple in your chin, your living will come in; a dimple in your cheek, your living's yours to seek." If you find someone you are working with, or going into business with, has a dimple in either place, quickly follow this procedure:

Place your finger (saucily) on your colleague's dimple and say: "By the luck which here is writ, Security shall grow a bit, And from the dimple in your (chin), Prosperity shall sure begin." Or "From the dimple in your (cheek), Luck and funds are ours to seek."

A dimple is a sign of great luck in business, so always keep an eye out for someone who has one; it will bring you great good fortune.

If you have a dimple yourself, touch it (or them) before you begin a money project: it will favor you with great success. Wishing upon your dimple is like having the touch of the fairy folk upon your face.

Four-leaf clover

This lucky emblem offers wonderful providence for business. It is regarded as important that you should simply find the clover, not go out looking for it.

If you are considering a new venture in business, and you find a four-leaf clover by chance on the eve of going into that venture, your proceedings will all pass off very fortuitously.

Take the clover leaf home and immediately place it next to a symbol of your new job, or business, or venture. Wish out loud that all your financial affairs will soon be "in clover." You should carry it with you in connection with that business, all the time.

If you have a clover leaf already and you want to wish for prosperity on a new undertaking, touch the second leaf from the top, counting clockwise: this is the leaf for wealth. Stroke the leaf and imagine your business, or financial power, blooming green and healthy.

Write your name, and that of your business or company, on a piece of quality paper, and light a golden-yellow candle beside it, with the leaf underneath. Let it burn for eight days.

Your venture will bloom, and money matters flow smoothly.

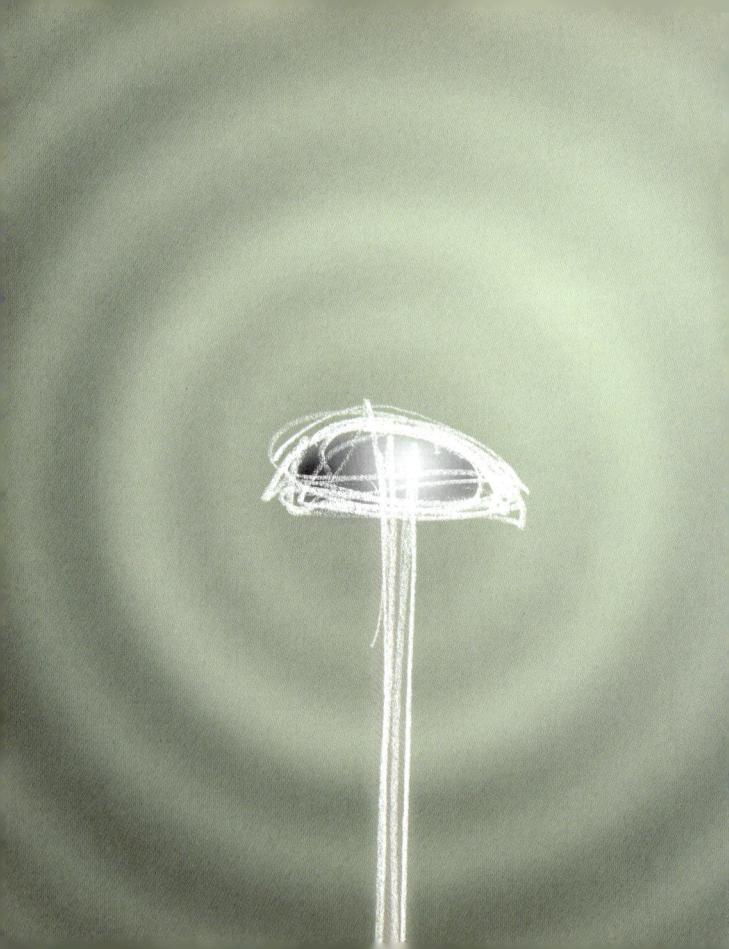

Pins

"He that will not stoop for a pin, will never be worth a dollar." So goes the old saying. If you find a pin, it is lucky in all matters; but for wealth:

Pick up the pin and kiss it three times.

Close your eyes and imagine the silver of the pin turning into silver in your pocket. Imagine light from the pin circling around you and bringing jangling coins.

Stick the pin into your jacket, or into your wallet; carry it around for the day.

When you go indoors, push the pin through some money-bills, and place it somewhere high.

Your luck with money will increase while you keep this talisman.

Coal

Despite the connotations of coal given to you at Christmas being for naughty children, coal in fact is a very lucky omen. If you find a piece of coal, or if someone gives you a piece:

Spit on the coal, and then burn it.

Burn a fragrant herb, or some incense (traditionally frankincense) with the coal in the fire: it will smell rich and wonderful.

As the coal burns and the fragrant smoke rises, make a wish for prosperity, which is strongly associated with coal. See more of everything in your imagination, rising out of the curls of smoke. Imagine more ease in your earning a living, but don't look for huge bags of gold. Coal is not a symbol of greed.

Your financial luck will surely be granted, and you should always be respectful of coal.

Salt

At the heart of a thousand lucky actions and superstitions, salt demands certain behavioral observations when it is spilled, passed, or given as a gift.

Plenty of salt in the house is a surety for plenty of money as well.

If you are short of funds, get someone to bring you a gift of salt; it should be given on a waxing moon, if possible.

When you receive salt, close your eyes and wish for prosperity. Taste some of the salt, and throw some in front of your feet.

Keep different salts in different places around the house; and when friends come to see you who are in need of a little luck with money, give them a little salt as well. In other words, spread the salt around.

Salt has always been regarded as a precious commodity, and your generosity and respect toward the salt will be rewarded with plenty in all things in your own life.

Rosemary

A very powerful herb, this has many applications for luck and in magic spells.

Hang a branch of rosemary at the door of your house, if you wish to have luck and plenty of money in your home life.

Take a small piece of the rosemary off this branch, and pop it into a glass of wine with which to toast the household and in particular a business you might just be beginning.

If you wish to be lucky with money on a specific occasion, take a piece of the rosemary from the door with you in your pocket.

Pin a sprig of rosemary on your coat if you go to the races, or to buy a ticket in a lottery or sweepstake. Luck will be on your side, but don't be greedy. Always give a few coins away when you have been favored.

Flowering wreaths

Hops are one of the best wreaths to make, but other flowers may be just as successful.

Tie either a bunch of flowering hops (they must be flowering) or another vinelike plant that is in flower (such as clematis, or jasmine, or wisteria) above a mirror in your home.

Make a wish for garlands of success in your business or money life.

Leave the bunch to dry for a year, until you can replace it with another made from fresh hops or flowers, to insure a year of prosperity and plenty of work to do.

Always touch the bunch for thanks when things go well financially.

Corn dolly

These are traditional ways of drawing down the power of the gods for fertility and plenty in the year to follow the grain harvest. Make your doll from anything you have on hand: it is extremely lucky if you make it from the last of anything you have been working with, such as the last trimmings of bread, or cookie dough, or (by tradition) the last wheat harvested in the field.

If your doll is made from growing things (grain, rosemary, herbs, grasses, lavender, etc.) make it as beautifully as you can, and tie it in places with green or golden-yellow ribbon. Use wire to get the shape right if need be.

If your doll is baked, decorate it carefully, and finish it with ribbons and pretty fabric.

Hang your doll up somewhere where it can remain, and on no account give it away. Wish on it every time you need special luck in business, or in finding extra money; the corn dolly brings luck to your work throughout the year.

Umbrellas

Mostly thought of as unlucky objects, umbrellas can turn your day to one of extraordinary good fortune. Here's how:

If someone near you drops an umbrella, make sure you say absolutely nothing, but quickly lean in to recover it for them.

This generous act on your part saves the owner from bad luck, but also means that you should have very good luck in anything concerning money.

Immediately go home and tape a pretty coin to the handle of your own umbrella. Ask out loud for "pennies from heaven," and wish, with your eyes closed, for a shower of money.

Within the week, money will come to you.

Stars

When you see a shooting star, of course, any wish can be granted you. If you wish to improve your finances, you should make the following spell:

As the star is shooting, close your eyes and say: "Money, pearls, and precious things will follow from a star with wings!" Blow the star a quick kiss, before it disappears.

When you go to work next day, or at home if you do some of your work from there, place a sticky silver or golden star on a piece of paper in front of you.

You will now have a very fortunate month for money, business, and everything connected with your work; it often brings a promotion.

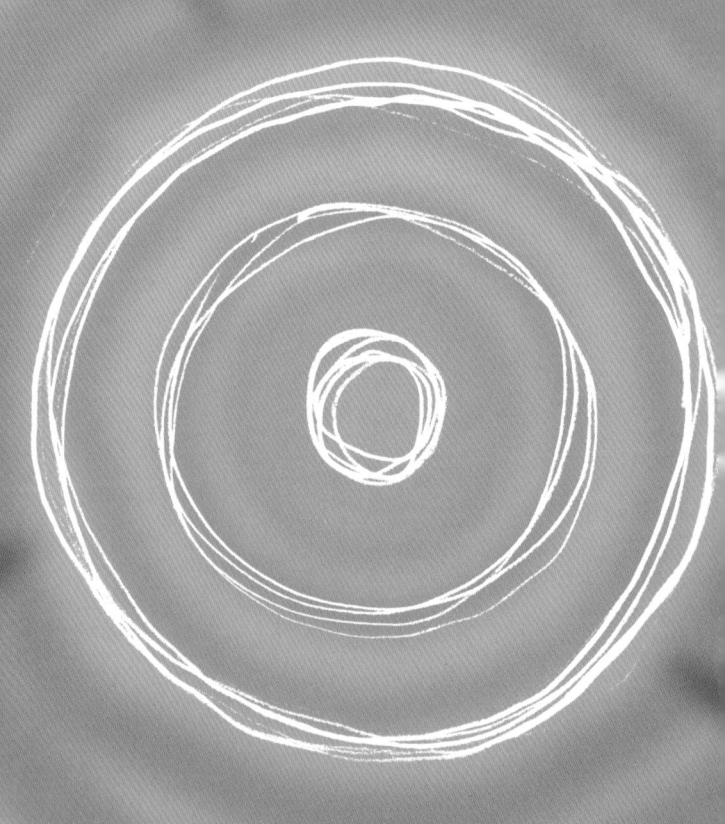

Wood

"Knock on wood" is something we all remember to say when we tempt providence in some way. Originally, this was a genuflection to the spirits that were believed to inhabit trees, although it also became associated with the idea of touching a piece of the "true cross." Witches still revere the spirits of trees, so here is a wishing ritual for the spirits of trees to bless our ventures.

When the first oak/ash/willow of the year is observed cloaked in its new green, touch the tree and utter a small prayer of thanks for renewed life. Then:

Quickly tie a piece of cord around the trunk and ask for new green shoots in your financial life. Remember, as Frost says, "Nature's first green is gold..."

Give the tree a libation, that is, a drink of ale, or water, or wine; and wish for plenty to eat and drink, and plenty of work to keep you busy, from the spring throughout the year.

Bow once to the tree, and leave it walking backward.

Your pocket should be made heavier, and work should flourish, as the tree gains more and more of its green. (Remember to say thank-you).

Wind

Sailors have great belief in the power of wind and offer the ocean a coin to make it blow. The other wishing spell concerning wind works the other way around:

If the wind suddenly and unexpectedly rises up, it may be a message from the gods. Turn fully around and look the wind in the face: let it blow through your hair.

Touch a coin in your purse or pocket and say: "Oh, Wind, the breath of deity, Please lend your power to uplift me."

Give the coin away to someone who needs it; but within a week, your gesture will have been rewarded manifold.

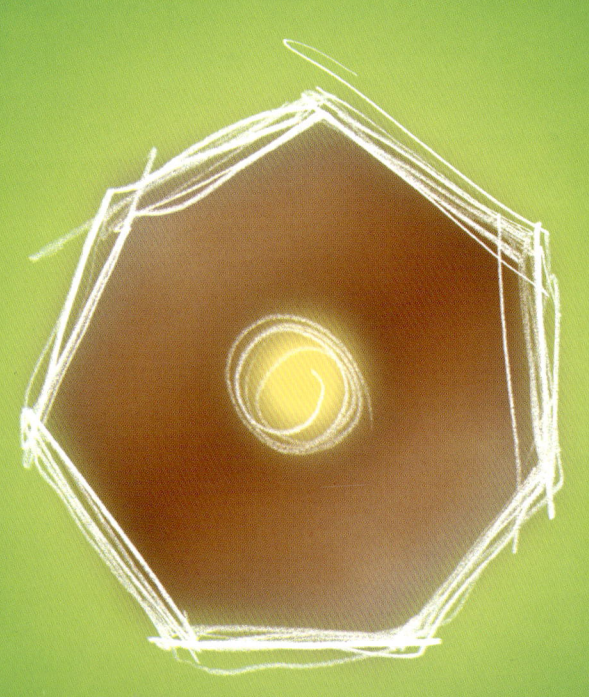

Coins

These are unmatchable as emblems of luck with money. Try the following:

If you are given an unusual coin by someone, or if you receive a new issue for the first time, turn it twice in your palm and whisper: "Little coin, grow a thousand fold; I pray my fortune soon to hold."

Take the coin home, being careful not to give it away on any account. Place it beside a candle of green or gold, and repeat the words.

Place the coin in a small pouch—blue, or green, or yellow, or red. Never spend it, but look to its growth in other terms.

Make sure to give away the value of the coin twice a year, to a friend or stranger who needs it. You will always, thus, have a little more than you need.

Itchy palm

The best-known sign of money coming in. Seize the moment to help it along a little.

When your palm itches, kiss it right in the spot the itch grows from.

Tie a yellow ribbon loosely around that same hand, though without making a bow: just loop it, and slip a small copper coin underneath the ribbon, against the itch.

Say: "Itchy palm where money comes, Bless me now with extra sums." Unslip the ribbon and take the coin to some water, where you should toss it.

If you now spend a little money, you will make even a little bit more.

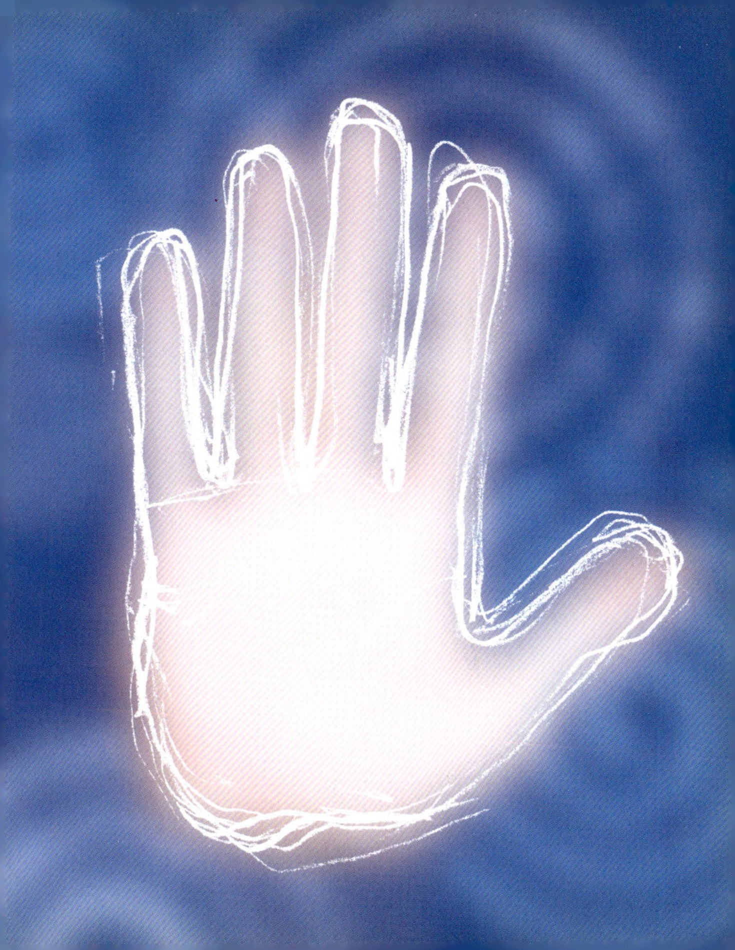

Marriage

To insure good material fortune in your marriage, you should do the following:

Inside the left wedding shoe, tape a small silver coin.

After the ceremony, place the coin with some of the rice or rose petals that have been thrown, and perhaps have caught in the bridal dress, in a pouch, or little purse.

On the first new moon after the wedding, show the coin to the light of the moon, and ask for silvery replenishment many times over.

Light a silver candle next to the coin for the first week of the growing moon, and treasure the silver coin. You will have luck with money in your married life.

Feathers

It is a sad soul who will pass by a feather without using this omen to spell for luck with money.

If you pass a feather on the grass, stop and lift it without a sound.

Push it into the soil where it lies, and push a tiny coin (like a penny) underneath it, for fairy treasure.

In exchange, the fairies will favor you for your kindness with treasure of your own.

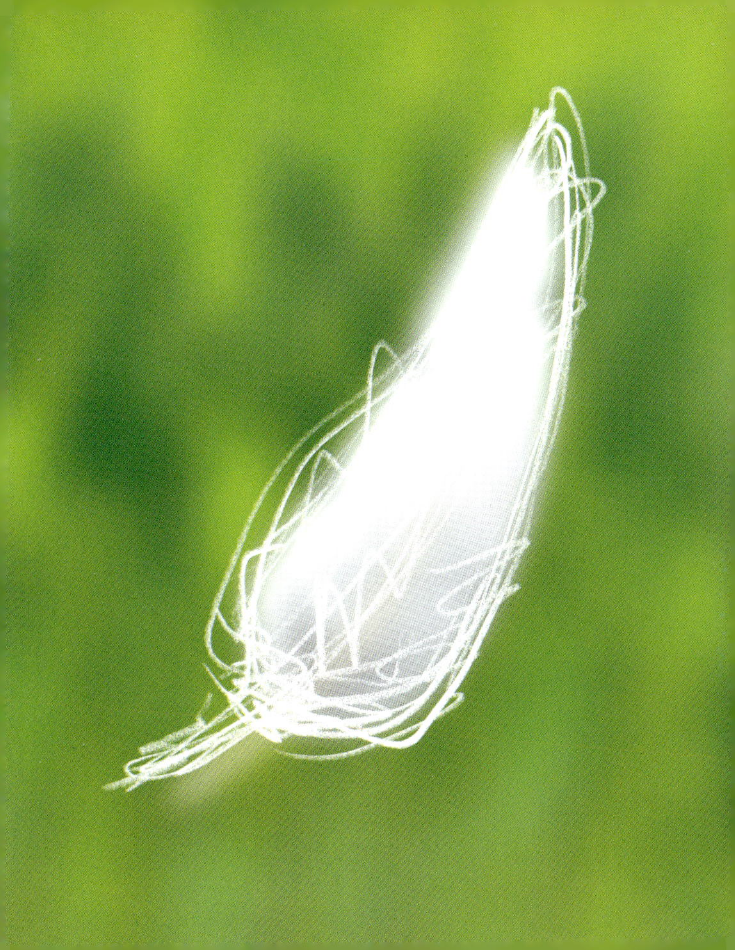

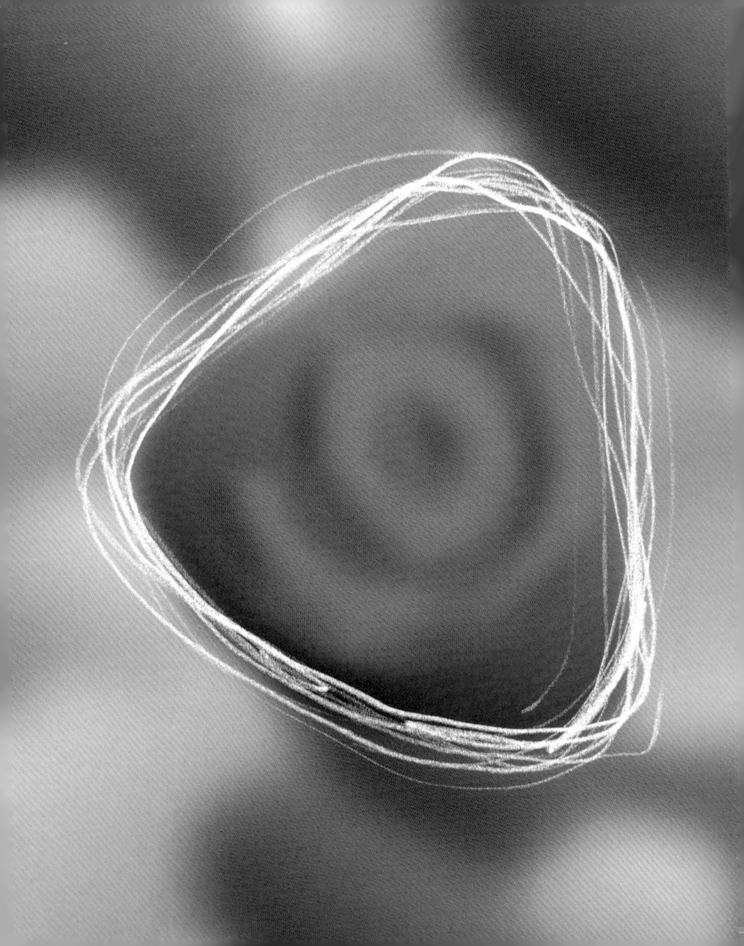

Fairy loaves

Beautiful fossils turned over on the sea-coast, or in the grounds of your home, are a wonderful omen—they are called "fairy loaves." If you are lucky enough to find one:

Lift the stone and instantly say "Thank you."

Standing where you are, turn three times on the spot, clockwise.

Take it home and clean it as though it were treasure. Place it on a mantelpiece, or on the stove. While it remains in your house, you should never want for bread.

Caress it from time to time, when your luck could do with a boost. Don't leave it outdoors—this would be to abuse fairy hospitality!

Cuckoo

Announcing the first days of Spring is not the only joy to be had from hearing a cuckoo sing.

When the first cuckoo is heard, be sure to have a penny in your pocket, which you must turn over. Change purses can be tipped out noisily in your pocket, or change jingled loudly. Make a strong wish at the same time for riches all the year.

If you don't have a penny or other coin, you must quickly run and fetch one; otherwise, you will miss your luck. Be sure to borrow from a friend and quickly return it, if this is closer at hand than home. On no account go without some change.

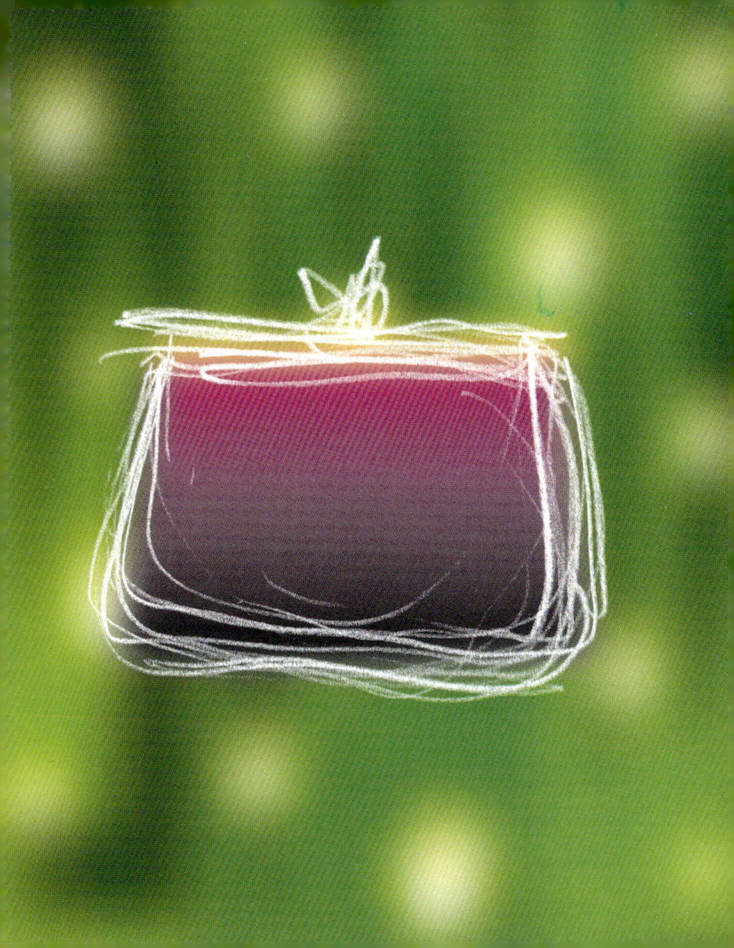

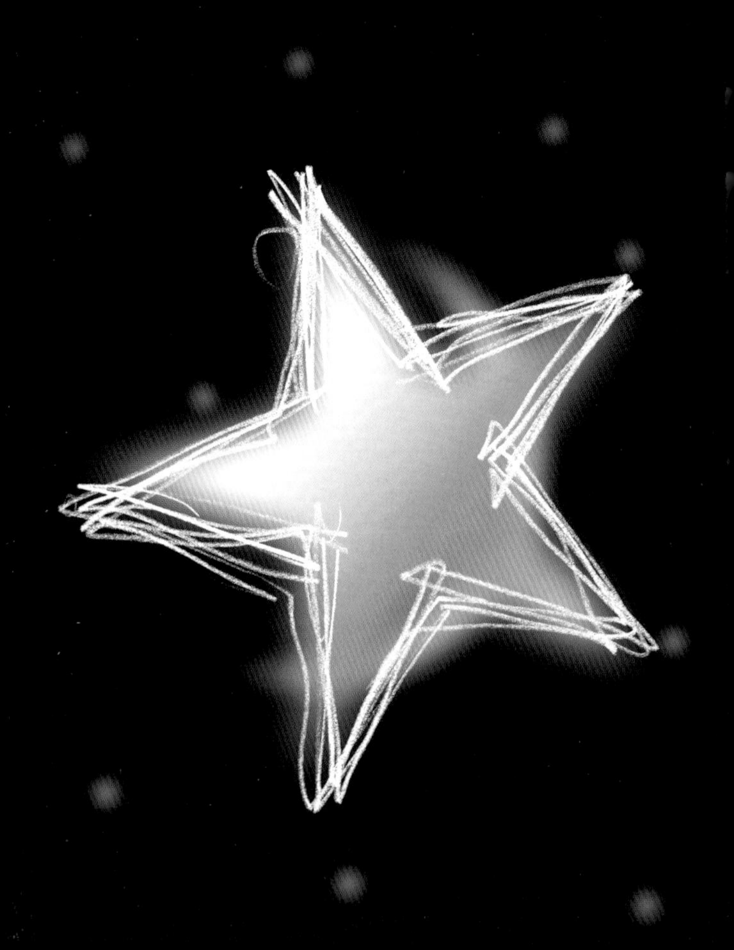

New Moon

A famous friend of wishers, it is very kind to those who ask for funds for a special purpose.

If you have a special thing you wish to buy, or pay for, go to the brand-new moon and hold up to it a piece of silver or a silver object. Some deem it best if this is a star-shaped object.

Wish very hard for what it is you want, and then say: "Welcome to thee, Lady Moon; May you bring my present very soon."

Repeat this three times, with a bow or curtsey to the moon each time. If the wish concerns money outright, turn a few coins in your pocket, and wish hard.

Within the month of the moon's sway, your fortunes should steadily wax, and your present either be given, or get much closer.

Bluebells

These are the homes of fairy folk, so you will be rewarded for making an offering to a bluebell.

In the first days of Spring when bluebells rise, make a journey, however far, to a place where bluebells grow.

Inhale the wonderful perfume from the flowers, and turn away from them; over your shoulder, toss a small coin—small enough for a fairy to carry.

Ask for just one bluebell in exchange for the coin; pick just one (and on no account more).

You will be lucky shortly, and money shall come to you "from out of the blue." To perpetuate the luck, cultivate a bluebell or blue hyacinth in a clay pot and push a coin underneath it. Tie a blue bow around the pot. Your fortunes will improve at work or with money.

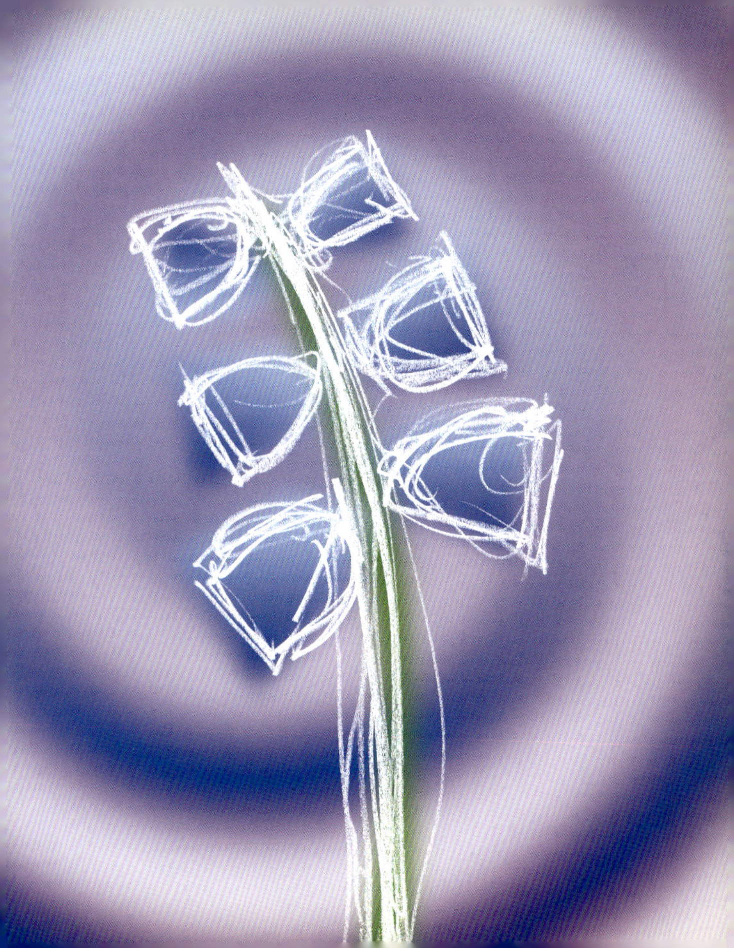

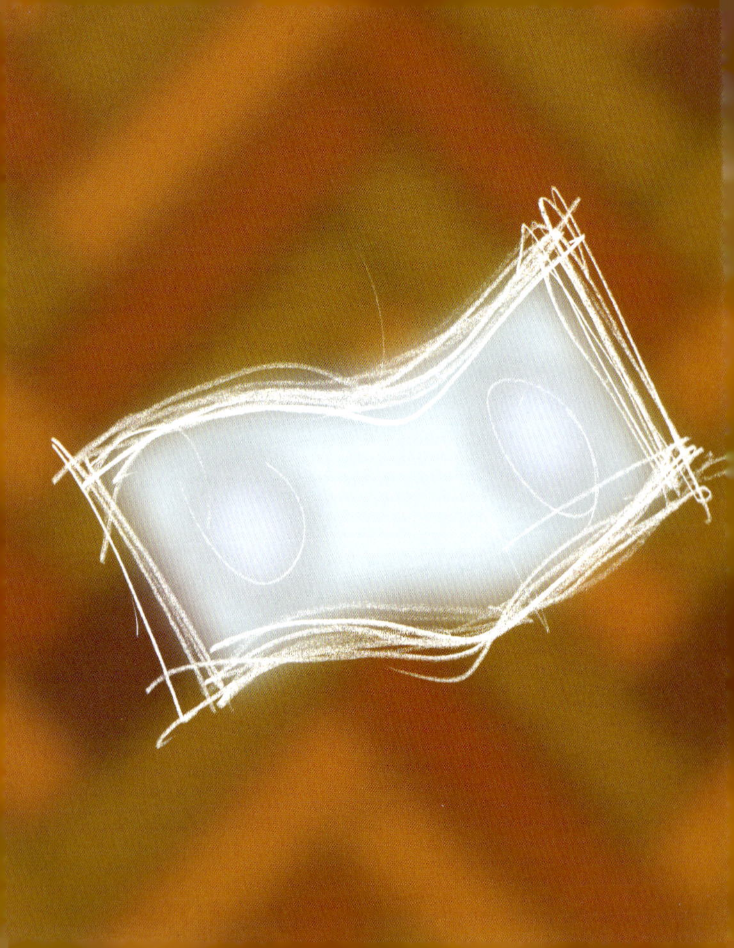

Dropping money

This is not a straightforward omen of loss: on the contrary, you can turn it to good luck.

When you drop a coin or bill on the floor, let someone else hand it back to you, so that money will pass through someone else's hands back to your own and thus reflect money received. It will be lucky for you, and for the other party.

Say together: "Money on the floor, money at my door," and link little fingers. Wish together for luck, seeing more money in the near future.

Place the dropped money somewhere special, and tie a ribbon around it (any color). Soon, money will come "through your door."

Purses

If a new purse appears, it must be treated correctly to be certain of a life without want.

If you give a purse or small bag to a friend as a gift, always place a new coin inside and explain it is not to be spent.

As you pass it over, make a wish for "like begets like"—that your sum will be returned many times in multiples.

When you change from an old purse to a new one, make sure you leave a coin in the purse you are putting away, so you are never without money. A purse with a coin inside is a lucky symbol, and you must wish on it: "Grant me prosperity, I shall not be greedy."

If you are given a purse without a coin inside, ask the giver for a small coin, and make a wish on it together as it brushes both of your hands.

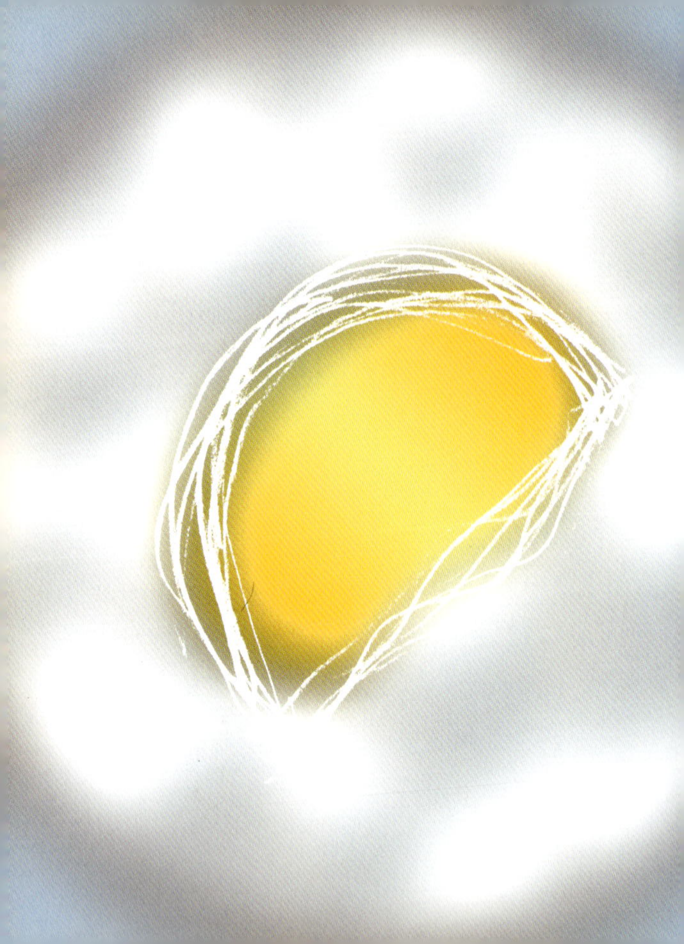

Lucky windfall

Here's what to do if you are lucky with money, to invite a repetition of the luck.

Take a coin of value (this used to be a sovereign) drawn from a sum of money you have won or been given unexpectedly.

Bury it deep in a bowl of sugar, and thank the goddess for the joyful present.

You will find you receive little sums at regular intervals; each time you do, you should remove the coin from the sugar and send it or give it to someone whose face will express joy.

In this manner you will receive, and give, plenty of joy and prosperity.

Spider

These creatures, who make beautiful webs, are symbols of industry and determination. The tiny reddish-brown ones are known as money spiders.

If a money spider crawls on your hand, be careful not to crush or hurt it. Make a prayer of thanks for its visit, and wish hard for money.

Go immediately and buy a ticket for a lottery or raffle, and remember not to be too demanding in the sums you anticipate.

When fortune replies with a win, make a pledge never to kill a spider.

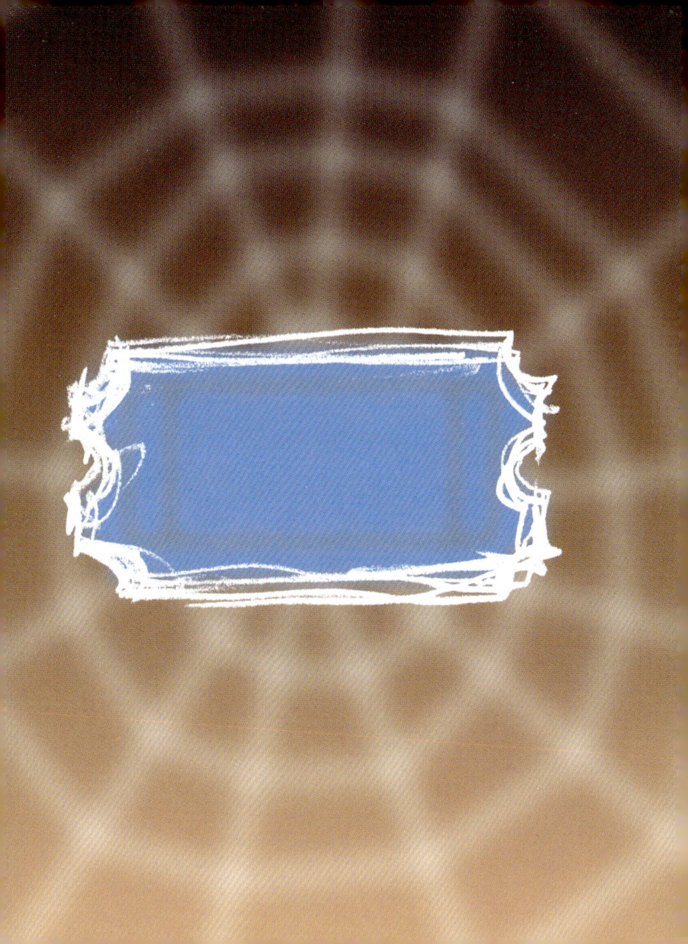

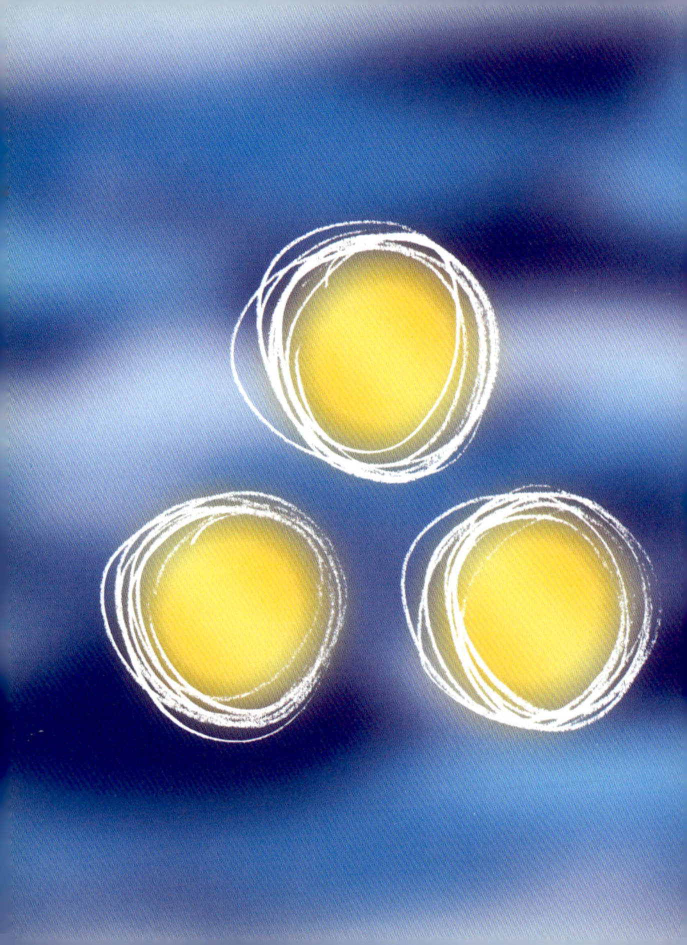

Three names

What to do if you meet two other people at a table, or in a room, with the same name as yours:

Link your hands together, make a wish for luck in business or with money, and close your eyes, still holding hands.

Write your name on paper and each of you pass the name to your namesake one place to your left. Then each of you should fold the paper up carefully and place it around a coin or small bill (of not too high a value). Each of you should exchange the same amount.

Pass the name and coin or bill one place again to the left, so that everyone has been given a name tag and money by the other two.

If later that day you go together and invest that money in a lucky gamble, you should make at least three times the amount back again.

Rainbow of prosperity

When you see a rainbow after a real storm, this wish-spell will turn an intensity of electric energy into a shower of good fortune so that you can find your pot of gold.

As soon as you see the rainbow, take out a coin (preferably silver) and hold it up to the arc. Trace the shape of the rainbow with the coin.

Tell the rainbow, which is deemed a sign of peace, that you wish to emerge from a financially stormy period. Press the coin between your palms, and imagine one palm filling up with more coins; then bow to the rainbow.

Go straight to a flower shop and buy an iris, the symbol of the rainbow. At home, or on your office desk, put the iris in a vase and place the coin next to it. Gather six other colored items (anything will do: candles, ribbons, flowers, fabric, photo frames, eyeglasses, etc.) so that all seven, including the iris, make up the colors of the rainbow; place them in proximity to the coin.

Leave them all together for seven days; after which you should have seven bonuses of money of whatever size or description.

Elephants

These are lucky, but feisty, symbols. The basic truth is that elephants must be appeased—otherwise, they go a little crazy. If you want an elephant to bring you trunks of money:

Buy a special elephant charm or ornament on the first day of a new venture or new job. It will work just as well if it is your first day of a course at a new college. But please note, the animal must have its trunk UP, not dangling down.

Place the elephant, however small, facing the door of your office or study, or whichever place you work. Rub the trunk and wish for blessings, and at the same time promise not to be mean with the money you earn.

Attend often to the position of the elephant: if it gets knocked down or turned around, make sure you replace it properly. It must always face the door.

Whenever you are lucky with money, place a few very small flowers at the elephant's feet, by way of thanks. Never forget—for the elephant will also never forget!

This edition first published in 2005 by
Quadrille Publishing Limited
Alhambra House
27-31 Charing Cross Road
London WC2H OLS

PUBLISHING DIRECTOR Anne Furniss
DESIGN Johnson Banks
PRODUCTION Vincent Smith, Funsho Asemota

© TEXT Titania Hardie 1999
© DESIGN AND LAYOUT Quadrille Publishing Limited 1999

All rights reserved. No part of this book may be reproduced in any manner whatsoever without permission in writing from the publisher

British Library Cataloguing in Publication Data
A catalogue record for this book is available
from the British Library

ISBN 1 84400 260 8

Printed in China